Letts

KS2

VISUAL
REVISION
GUIDE

SUCCESS

English

Author

Lynn Huggins-Cooper

CONTENTS

SPEAKING AND LISTENING

READING

WRITING

TEST, ANSWERS AND GLOSSARY

SAY IT OUT LOUD!

WHAT IS SPEAKING AND LISTENING?

Part of your *English Programme of Study* at school is *Speaking and Listening*. This is to help you to *organise your thoughts* to make speeches, to *speak effectively* to an audience, to *listen to ideas* and to *be persuasive*. It seems silly when you think about it – you learned to speak and listen when you were a toddler!

The way you speak and the *way you are able to explain things* does affect the way that people see you – so it is worth spending some time *thinking about how to present your ideas* and thoughts in the best possible way!

I LOVE reading out loud to the class!

You love the sound of your own voice...!

4

READING ALOUD WITH CONFIDENCE

There are some easy tips you can follow to make reading aloud less of an ordeal!

- Imagine that you are *reading to a younger brother or sister* rather than the whole class. Try to *forget about your audience*.

- Read *slowly and calmly*. When you are nervous, it is easy to rush and then you are more likely to make mistakes.

- *Take notice of full stops and commas* – they give you a chance to *pause and take a breath*.

- *Practise at home* in front of your family – or even in front of the mirror!

- If your *throat feels tight* and your *mouth feels dry*, because you are nervous, pretend to yourself that your tongue has become *incredibly heavy* (without making daft faces!). This will *relax you* before you start to read.

★ top tip ★

Remember – do not fidget! If you twiddle your hair or pull at your collar, people will know you are nervous – and you will feel even worse!

QUICK TEST

1. Why is Speaking and Listening part of the school curriculum?

2. Why is it important to think about how you present your ideas?

HAVE A GO ...

Listen to people on the television reading the news – think about it, they are staying calm in front of MILLIONS of people! Practise reading aloud from the newspaper to your family – be a newsreader!

LISTENING AND PRESENTING

You may get told *lots of times* by your teachers and parents that arguing is a bad thing. English is great – you are expected to argue – but *not* about who is the most gorgeous soap star or who should be number one in the charts!

In English lessons, you will be expected to *develop skills in listening* to the views of other people and *presenting your own arguments*. Sometimes you will be given a topic – *often a question* – to think about. It could be:

* Should fox-hunting be banned?

* Should mobile phones be allowed in class?

* Should we all be vegetarian?

* Should school uniforms be abolished?

You should think about how you *feel about the issue* and then compare your ideas with friends. *Sharing views* makes it easier to come up with *good arguments*.

DRAMATIC DEBATES!

BEING A GOOD LISTENER

When you listen to the opposing team's ideas, you should be *quiet and sensible*. A <u>debate</u> is not a free-for-all shouting match! You should *make quick notes* of things people say that you disagree with – you might want to *respond to their ideas* in your own speech. It is hard to do this at first, but like everything, it gets easier with practice.

Make sure you are clear about which are the *main points* of their argument. You must reply to these, so that the audience that is listening decides you have the *stronger argument*.

PRESENTING YOUR OWN IDEAS

Discuss your viewpoint with your team. Sharing ideas is the best way to get organised! Try to think about the things the other team will say, so that you can have your answers ready.

If you are given time, do some research on your argument and find quotations from important people to back up your ideas – perhaps someone has written a report or a book on your topic. Look in the library and on the Internet.

Make notes, then re-read them and pick out the most important points. Practise remembering what these are – perhaps make up a mnemonic (a silly sentence using the first letter of each word you want to remember) to help you.

Perhaps I can talk Mum into giving me more pocket money!

Think about it carefully first or she might talk you into taking less!

★ top tip ★

Teachers can sometimes be sneaky and ask you to prepare a speech in favour of something you don't like – such as school dinners or uniform – or they can ask you to argue against something you love, like watching TV. They are not being mean – they are just helping you to become a great speaker!

HAVE A GO ...

Does your school, youth club or local Teacher's Centre have a debate team? If you enjoy presenting arguments and trying to persuade people to come round to your way of thinking, debates can be great fun!

QUICK TEST

Make notes for a speech in favour of using mobile phones at school. Remember to think about any arguments people may have against you, so you have a reply ready. Then present your ideas to an audience – your family or even your class at school!

7

WHAT DOES A RESEARCHER DO?

Research, of course! Lots of people do research every day, at school and at work. If you were doing a history project about Vikings, you would look in the library and on the Internet for information. Researchers do the same thing to find out information about the topics they are working on.

If you were a magazine researcher, one of your jobs would be to find out about topics for articles. You would look in books and on the Internet, but you would also look in newspapers and magazines. You could also find out about people's views by doing interviews. This means asking people questions.

BE A RESEARCHER!

BE A RESEARCHER!

Imagine you are a researcher for TeenScene, a magazine for teenagers. It includes articles on music, fashion, TV/film and extreme sports like parascending. You are going to do some research for an article. Choose from:

- **SHARK ATTACK!**

- **GOING VEGETARIAN – HOW TO BREAK IT TO YOUR PARENTS!**

- Have you got what it takes to be a pop star?

- **SNOWBOARDING – FAD OR SPORT?**

SOURCES OF INFORMATION

Use the following *sources of information* to *research the article* you want to write:

* Books
* Magazines
* Newsletters
* News groups on the Internet
* Information from special groups such as a sports club or conservation group
* Interviews with friends and family
* Television programmes
* Videos
* Radio programmes and interviews

Now write the article!

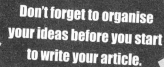

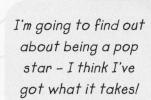

★ **top tip** ★

Don't forget to organise your ideas before you start to write your article.

I'm going to find out about being a pop star – I think I've got what it takes!

Only if all you need is a bad voice and dirty clothes!

9

TEST ROUND-UP

LET'S ARGUE!

You are going to plan a <u>debate</u> *in favour of school uniform* – and that could be hard, if you don't like wearing it!

<u>Brainstorm</u> your ideas. *Make a note* of things to do with wearing school uniform – *for* and *against*.

Think about these questions:

> Is uniform *more* or *less* expensive than ordinary clothes?

> Does uniform help to make people *look the same* – and is that a good thing?

> Is uniform smart? Is being smart important?

> What do kids wear *at home*?

★ **top tip** ★

Watch people on the news or on current affairs programmes – you can often see debates and arguments.

GET ORGANISED!

Organise your ideas into arguments for and against school uniform. Arranging the information in a 'for' and 'against' table may be useful.

Don't forget to do some research for your debate. You may find articles in old newspapers or magazines to support you. Back issues (old copies) of papers and magazines can be found in the public library. You could also look on the Internet.

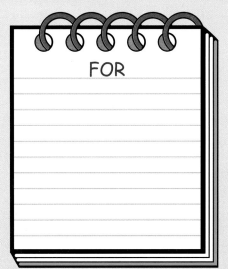

FOR

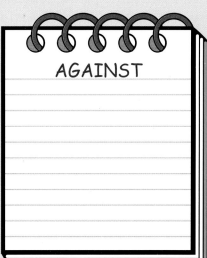

AGAINST

DEBATE!

Present your argument to an audience. You could do this at home – ask your parents to argue against school uniform, especially if they believe you should wear it! You could also ask your teacher if you could present your arguments to the class.

All this arguing is great fun – but I don't like having to think so hard!

No, you just like the shouting!

DO YOU LIKE READING?

We read things *every day* – signs, cereal packets, labels, text messages, magazines, newspaper, books – it's all reading! But what do you read *for pleasure*?

Do you only read books at *school*, because your teacher tells you to? Then you don't know what you're missing! Do you ever go to the *library*? It's not just a place to find books for school work – you can find a whole world of *exciting stories* – and it's *all free*!

But how do you decide which *book* to read?

BOOK POWER!

THE BLURB

Do you make a habit of reading <u>blurbs</u>? A blurb is the writing on the *back of a book* that tells you briefly *what's inside*. It tells you about the *main characters* and the situations that they find themselves in, but *leaves you hanging* so that you want to *read more* – which is the whole point of a blurb!

The pictures on the *cover* of a book can also affect whether you want to read it. Publishers spend huge amounts of money on *artwork* for the covers of books for that reason.

Do you choose books because they are of a particular <u>genre</u>? That means a *particular category* of books such as adventures, thrillers, horror, romance etc. What genre is your favourite?

BOOK REVIEWS

Have you ever written a book review at school? Which book did you review? Why did you choose it? Book reviews can be boring and deadly if you are just doing them because you have to. But why not write a review as though you were a journalist, writing for a magazine? Reviewers write about books, films and plays, to tell other people about them, so they can decide what to read and watch.

Pick a book that you have really enjoyed. If you love a story, you will be able to persuade other people that they should read it, because your enthusiasm will show in the words you choose.

I like sci-fi books the best – but I thought a blurb was a monster from outer space!

No, that's your reflection, silly!

★ **top tip** ★

Make sure you read a variety of books. The more you read, the better your own writing will be.

QUICK TEST

1. What have you read today?
2. What is a genre?
3. What is a blurb?

ANSWERS: **2.** A category of writing. **3.** A summary of the plot of a book.

HAVE A GO ...

Look in newspapers and magazines and read reviews – it can help you to develop your own style of writing.

BETWEEN THE LINES

READING BETWEEN THE LINES

Have you ever heard someone say that they have found something out by *reading between the lines*? It means that they have looked behind the *obvious meaning* of the words to find the *true meaning*.

When you read a book, you should *read between the lines* to see if there is a *hidden meaning*. Sometimes authors try to give us *messages about important things*, but the messages are hidden away in the stories.

Have you ever read any stories by Anne Fine? She writes excellent stories, mostly about teenagers. She wrote a book called *Flour Babies* that seemed to be about a school science project, but reading between the lines it is about *fatherhood and how responsibilities change people*.

IMPORTANT MESSAGES

Authors sometimes write books by *starting with the message they want to give* and weaving a story around it.

Dinosaurs and All That Rubbish by Michael Foreman seems, at first look, to be a funny book about dinosaurs, but if you read between the lines the message is about *saving the world from pollution*.

Other books carry messages warning us against things. *Journey to Jo'burg* by Beverley Naidoo seems to be about a family, but it carries a message about *how racism is wrong* and people should not be judged according to the colour of their skin.

★ **top tip** ★

If you are writing a book review and you talk about messages you have found by reading between the lines, always refer back to the part of the story that you think gave you the message. This will help you to earn the highest marks possible!

14

HIDDEN MEANINGS

Stories with hidden meanings and messages:

- *Piggybook* by Anthony Browne
- *Goggle Eyes* by Anne Fine
- *Freaky Friday* by Mary Rodgers
- *The Lion, the Witch and the Wardrobe* by C.S. Lewis
- *The Iron Woman* by Ted Hughes
- *Wolf* by Gillian Cross
- *My Mate Shofiq* by Jan Needle

Read the books and see if you can find the true meanings by reading between the lines!

I've just read The Lion and the Witch in the Wardrobe. It was great!

Wasn't it rather dark, trying to read in a wardrobe?

QUICK TEST

1. What does reading between the lines mean?

2. Have you ever read a book with a message or a hidden meaning?

HAVE A GO ...

See if you can find a collection of different books, all linked by a message – perhaps about the environment, relationships, honesty – whatever you like!

ANSWER: 1. Looking beyond the obvious meaning of words.

A RIOTOUSLY GOOD READ!

WHAT IS A GOOD BOOK?

When you *finish a storybook*, people often say to you "Was it good?" The question is, *how do you know*?

Of course, whether a book is good or not *can mean many things* to many different people. If you enjoy a book, you think it is good. *Your opinion* is affected by whether the book was about something you *found interesting*. Someone else might read the book, because you said it was exciting, and *be disappointed* because it was not about a subject that they found interesting. Whatever subject a book is about, there are certain ingredients that make a storybook easier and *more interesting* to read.

A good strong story line

An exciting beginning

A strong – and even surprising – ending

Believable, realistic characters

When you finish reading a good book, you feel as though you want to know more. The characters *become so real* to you that you want to know more about their adventures. If you are really lucky, the author writes a <u>sequel</u> or even a series! Have you ever enjoyed a story *that much*?

★ **top tip** ★
If you like books by a particular author, do an Internet search to find out more about the author and the books they write.

The time travel story sounds great. I could make myself ten years older so you couldn't boss me around!

I like the idea of ghost stories, they might give me ideas on how to scare you!

SOME GOOD READS

When you read a book, make a few notes to remind yourself how you felt after reading it. Did you want to read more? Here are some good reads to look out for:

Other worlds

His Dark Materials – a <u>trilogy</u> of fabulous books by Phillip Pullman.

The Narnia Chronicles by C.S. Lewis –- full of fantastic characters.

The Weirdstone of Brisingamen by Alan Garner – has you breathless with suspense!

Adventure stories

I Am David by Anne Holm – a boy on an epic journey across Europe to find his family.

The Machine Gunners by Robert Westall – a boy who finds a crashed Heinkel war plane during the Second World War – complete with machine gun.

A Handful of Time by Kit Pearson – an excellent story of time travel.

Animals

I, Houdini by Lynn Reid Banks – hilarious stories of a 'self-educated hamster'.

The Black Stallion by Walter Farley – the adventures of a boy and his horse.

Island of the Blue Dolphins by Scott O'Dell – the adventures of a girl alone on an island and the animals she encounters.

HAVE A GO ...

Ask your friends and family to recommend books to you. After reading them, talk about the story and compare ideas. You may be amazed at how different your views are!

QUICK TEST

What ingredients does a book need to be a good read?

ANSWER: A good strong story line, an exciting beginning, a strong – and even surprising – ending, believable, realistic characters.

17

FICTION vs NON-FICTION

WHAT IS FICTION?

Fiction is writing which is made up by the author. Imaginary stories are fiction.

There are certain features that fiction books share:

- Fast, flowing text that you read quickly to find out what will happen next in the story.

- You read it from the beginning to the end – rather than dipping in and out – or you lose the sense of the story.

- The author's style can be very personal – as though they are talking straight to you, the reader.

- Fiction for older readers is not usually illustrated as the author relies on the words to weave a picture.

- You can often work out the meaning of new, unfamiliar words from the setting and what happens before or after in the story.

I like reading non-fiction – especially books about sharks and alligators – terrors of the deep!

I like reading fiction about girls defeating their annoying brothers!

WHAT IS NON-FICTION ?

<u>Non-fiction</u> writing is information, not made-up stories. Books that tell us about history, science, the natural world and other countries are mostly non-fiction. They contain lots of *true facts*. These are the sort of books you use when you are doing a project at school. This book is non-fiction, for example.

There are certain features that non-fiction books share:

* People often *dip into non-fiction for information*, rather than reading it from cover to cover.

* There are usually *illustrations* – including tables, diagrams and photographs – to accompany the words and to help explain things.

* *Specialised vocabulary* – special words used only for *particular subjects* – often appears, so non-fiction books often have a <u>glossary</u>.

* The author's style is often *impersonal* – reporting and describing things.

* People often read non-fiction quickly, *skimming through* to find information they need and then re-reading the relevant sections carefully.

★ top tip ★

Try to remember the differences between fiction and non-fiction – you will be expected to know them for your SATs. But remember that sometimes it's hard to tell, because people often write fiction based on real facts and events.

QUICK TEST

1. Name three common features of fiction.

2. Name three common features of non-fiction.

3. What is a glossary?

ANSWERS: **1. and 2.** See above. **3.** A dictionary of specialised vocabulary.

HAVE A GO ...

Keep a log of books you use and read through the week. Which do you use most: fiction or non-fiction?

WHOSE STORY?

WHO IS THE AUTHOR?

The author of a piece is the person who wrote it. Sometimes, they write with their own voice – that means that they are writing about their own feelings and experiences. If you were writing your autobiography – the story of your life – it would all be written in your voice, because it happened to you.

> On a Saturday morning, when I was a child, my dad would take my sister and I to the open market along Sydney Street. The smells, colours and sounds stay with me to this day! I would buy a huge bag of sherbet-filled chews from the market and then dive into David's Books in search of the comic books I craved. *Tales of the Unexplained, Astounding Stories* – I loved them all!

That passage is written in the author's own voice, because she is writing about herself.

I wonder who would play me if they filmed my autobiography ...?

It would have to be a funny, clumsy, scruffy person ...!

20

WHO IS A NARRATOR?

The <u>narrator</u> is the *storyteller*. The narrator may be the author, but is often a *character within the story*. The narrator does not usually speak with the author's voice, but with his or her own voice.

Read the passage below.

I started my life lonely and unwanted. I scavenged for food on rubbish tips and in bins. When it was cold, I froze. When it was wet, the rain pounded on my unsheltered back. One day, I smelled the mouth-watering aroma of meat in gravy. I ran to the food, cramming it into my mouth. I heard a clang and realised I was trapped in a cage!

After a terrible journey, I found myself in the darkness of a strange-smelling stone building. I heard a noise and one of The Hated Ones came. I hid, expecting a blow, but she brought food and murmured soft words to me.

The passage above is written from the *point of view of a feral cat*, taken in by a family. Obviously, the cat could not be the author – they would find it hard to hold a pen! But the cat's character is the narrator of the passage.

★top tip★

Make sure you can use words like narrator and author when you are writing – it will help you to sound knowledgeable, and you will get higher marks!

QUICK TEST

1. What is a narrator?

2. What is an autobiography?

ANSWERS: **1.** A storyteller. **2.** The story of the author's life.

HAVE A GO ...

Next time you read a book, think about whose voice is telling the story – the author, or a narrator?

INCREDIBLE IMAGERY!

IMAGERY

Imagery is about making images or pictures in your mind's eye. It makes pieces of work more exciting because of the vivid descriptions. You will come across three main types of imagery:

- ◆ Similes
- ◆ Metaphors
- ◆ Personification

SIMILES

Similes describe things by saying they are like something else.

The cat was as fluffy as a dandelion clock.

The old man's face was as wrinkly as elephant skin.

The moth danced around the lamp like a prima ballerina.

The monkey scratched her head, looking like a puzzled child.

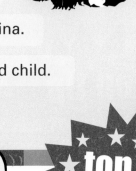

I'm as strong as metal!

Yeah – but as wet as a fish ...

★ top tip ★

If a description uses the words 'like' or 'as' (something) it is called a simile.

METAPHORS

Metaphors describe things by saying they *are* something else.

The slug *was* a rubber tube, lying on the path.

The newt *was* a tiny dragon, lurking behind a rock.

The baby *was* a siren, sounding in the night.

The blackberry *was* a jewel, shining in the sun.

PERSONIFICATION

Personification describes things by giving *human characteristics* to *non-human* things.

The *tree was a tall dancer,* her green skirt swirling in the breeze.

Winter is a wicked old man, pinching children's cheeks with his cold fingers.

My tiredness cuddled me to sleep, like my mother's arms.

The shadows *followed me, like an assassin* in a dark cloak.

HAVE A GO ...

When you are reading – books, magazines, advertisements – look for imagery. Make a note of any really good examples and use them to help you to make your own work more exciting.

QUICK TEST

1. What is a simile?

2. What is a metaphor?

3. What is meant by personification?

ANSWERS: 1. A simile describes something by saying it is LIKE something else. **2.** A metaphor describes something by saying it is actually IS something else. **3.** Personification gives human characteristics to things that are not human.

23

SOUND EFFECTS

ONOMATOPOEIA

<u>Onomatopoeia</u> means words that sound like the things they describe:

Smash   Bang   Clang   Pop   Fizz   Crunch   Flash

ALLITERATION

<u>Alliteration</u> is where the consonant sounds in words are repeated:

Beautiful Bethany baked bagels, buns and bread for breakfast.

The 'b' sound is repeated and the sentence is full of alliteration (and baked goods!)

Betty burped boldly, brandishing bright blue bottles.

Tongue-twisters often use alliteration – and the *repetition of words* – and that's why they are so tricky! Try:

Dopey Dave didn't dry dishes, Dopey Dave detested drying up.

Try making up some alliterative tongue-twisters of your own.

★ **top tip** ★

Make sure you can use words like alliteration and onomatopoeia when you are asked to talk about poems – it will win you extra marks.

Sam rhymes with 'bam!' and 'wham!' – Cool!

QUICK TEST

1. Which of these words are onomatopoeic?

   crown drip flower squash tape splash

2. Which words would fill the gaps to make these sentences alliterate?

   Saucy Susie drank sipped gargled soda slowly.

   Greedy Grant grabbed took pinched Gordon's grapes.

   Happy Harvey wished hoped thought he'd have help.

   Tabitha tasted nine ten eleven tiny treats.

ANSWERS: **1.** Drip, squash, splash. **2.** Sipped, grabbed, hoped, ten.

AWFUL AMBIGUITY!

WHAT IS AMBIGUITY?

Ambiguity is a difficult word – but when teachers are marking work they find lots of it! Ambiguity means that the meaning of a sentence is unclear. Read this sentence:

> The girl put the cat out, because she was noisy.

What does it mean? Did the girl put the cat out, because the cat was noisy, or did the girl put the cat out, because the girl was noisy? The meaning of the sentence is unclear, so it is an ambiguous sentence.

top tip

Always read your work back to yourself when you have finished, to check that your meanings are clear. What seems clear when you write it does not always seem so clear when you read it!

How about, "The dog sniffed the bin, because it was smelly."

The only smelly thing around here is you!

26

SPOT THE REAL MEANING!

Read these sentences – what do you think the writer meant in each case?

The dog chased the cat, because it was bored.

The cat or the dog – which was bored? Was the dog trying to cheer the cat up, because she was bored, or was the dog looking for mischief because it was bored?

The teacher scolded the girl, because she was being nasty.

The teacher or the girl – who was nasty? Was the teacher telling the girl off, because she was a horrible, grumpy teacher, or was the girl moaning at the teacher, because the girl was being naughty?

The mother cuddled her baby, because she was crying.

Who was crying – the mother or the baby?

It's important to *make your meaning clear*! Imagine if you said, "If that cat doesn't want her food, throw it away," and your Mum *threw the cat in the bin ...*!

QUICK TEST

Re-write these sentences so that the meanings are clear.

1. The hedgehog ate the slug, because it was hungry.

2. The cat chased the hamster, because it was naughty.

3. The girl picked up the cat, because she was lost.

ANSWERS: 1. Because it was hungry, the hedgehog ate the slug. 2. Because it was naughty, the cat chased the hamster. 3. Because the cat was lost, the girl picked it up.

HAVE A GO ...

Sometimes meaning becomes unclear because the sentence you are writing goes on and on and on and on ... It is better sometimes to use shorter sentences to make your meanings clear.

27

SPECIAL WORDS

English has special vocabulary all of its own – words that you need to learn, so you can talk about them. The words on this page are to do with reading. You will already know that an author is a person who writes books and an illustrator is a person who draws the pictures. You will also know that books have a title – what they are called. But did you know that a book has an ISBN? It stands for International Standard Book Number and is used by bookshops and libraries.

ISBN

SPECIAL WORDS

FOOTNOTES AND PARENTHESIS

These are special words that give the reader extra information about what they are reading.

Footnotes are found at the foot, or bottom, of the page. Footnotes are used to explain hard words in a piece of writing. Sometimes they are used to give the reader extra information.

Parenthesis means words that are added in brackets to a piece of writing to give us more information.

Sometimes words in parenthesis are explanations:

• The boy (who had already been to the shop) said he would go to buy the milk.

Sometimes words in parenthesis are afterthoughts:

• I will be on the football team this year! (I hope ...)

MORE SPECIAL WORDS

Appendix

An appendix is a collection of extra information added at the end of a book. If a book was about insects, the appendix could have information about which flowers to plant to attract butterflies.

Glossary

A glossary is a collection of words. You find them in <u>non-fiction</u> books. There is a glossary in this book. All the words, that are difficult to understand, are highlighted in bold print, to show that they are in the glossary. The meanings of the words are given, so you can learn new words.

Index

The index is a list of words, found at the back of a book, which tells you which page contains the things you are looking for. They are arranged in alphabetical order to make finding things easier.

★ **top tip** ★
Make sure you look at the glossary in this book – it will tell you about lots of words you need to know!

Do you think I'll be mentioned in the glossary?

No, I don't think the word annoying is listed!

QUICK TEST

1. What is an ISBN?

2. What is a footnote?

HAVE A GO ...

Can you explain to someone how to use an index?

THE STORY OF A LIFE!

SPECIAL TYPES OF TEXT

You may have heard these words before:

* Curriculum Vitae (CV)   * Biography   * Autobiography

All these special types of text tell us about people's lives.

A <u>Curriculum Vitae</u> is a record of what exams people have passed, what other qualifications they have and what jobs they have done. People use them when they are applying for jobs.

Read this <u>CV</u>:

Name:	Sheila Huggins
Education:	School Leaving Certificate
Work:	Hassans Jewellers until birth of son, Stephen in 1953 Own business as jeweller 1970 – 1983 Agar's Jewellers 1983 – retirement in 1999

BIOGRAPHIES

A <u>biography</u> is the story of someone's life.

Sheila Huggins left school as soon as she was allowed to – not because she wanted to, but because she had to earn a living. She was lucky and was taken on as an apprentice at Hassans, a renowned jewellery workshop, where she learned her trade. She worked, like so many other women at the time, until she had her son, Stephen. Sheila used her talents to earn money at home, running her own business until 1983, when her youngest daughter started senior school. Sheila carried out many amazing pieces of work, including repairs to a Witch Doctor's neckpiece – reputed to curse her if she did a bad job! – and the famous pearl and sapphire necklace worn by Diana, Princess of Wales, in her engagement photographs.

AUTOBIOGRAPHIES

An <u>autobiography</u> is the story of someone's life, written by the person themselves.

I left school as soon as I was allowed to – not because I wanted to, but because I had to earn a living. I was lucky and was taken on as an apprentice at Hassans, a renowned jewellery workshop, where I learned my trade. I worked, like so many other women at the time, until I had my son, Stephen. I used my skills to earn money at home, running my own business until 1983, when my youngest daughter started senior school. I carried out many interesting pieces of work, including repairs to a Witch Doctor's neckpiece – reputed to curse me if I did a bad job! – and the famous pearl and sapphire necklace worn by Diana, Princess of Wales, in her engagement photographs.

★ top tip ★

To make sure you know the difference between a CV, biography and autobiography, have a go at writing your own. You should be able to talk about each type.

I think I shall write my autobiography.

Huh! A book about eating, shouting and watching television!

HAVE A GO ...

Can you see the differences between the CV, biography and the autobiography? They all tell us about the same things, but in different ways.

QUICK TEST

1. What is an autobiography?

2. What is a biography?

3. What is CV short for?

ANSWERS: **1.** A book about your own life. **2.** A book about someone else's life. **3.** Curriculum Vitae.

31

MAKING SENSE

COMPREHENSION SKILLS

Comprehension means understanding. When you do a comprehension exercise at school, it tests whether you have understood what you have read. In your Key Stage Two SATs, you will have a comprehension exercise as part of your reading test.

You need to read the passage you are given carefully before trying to answer any questions.

★ top tip ★
You should use quotations from the text to support your answers – it will help you to gain more marks!

SKIMMING, SCANNING AND KEY WORDS

Skimming means reading through a passage quickly to find out what it is about.

Scanning is done after you have read the article through once and have read the questions. You scan or sweep the text, looking for words that are linked to the questions.

These are called key words and they will help you to find the facts you need, so you can answer the questions.

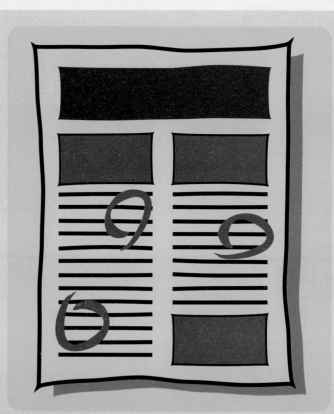

STRATEGIES FOR ANSWERING

Read this passage:

> The ladybird lays yellow eggs, like tiny rugby footballs. When the young ladybirds hatch, their skin is like black rubber. They look nothing like their parents! Ladybirds eat aphids, which are tiny flies that feed by sucking sap from plants. Gardeners welcome ladybirds to the garden because they help to kill these pests.

Question:

> What do ladybirds eat?

Firstly read the passage. Then read the question and decide which is the key word. The key word in this question is eat. So scan the text and find the word – and you will be able to answer the question.

Answer:

> Ladybirds eat aphids.

Ugh, I don't fancy eating flies!

Who knows what the dinner ladies are feeding us!

QUICK TEST

1. What do we mean by key words?

2. How do we scan text to find answers?

3. What do we mean by skim?

HAVE A GO ...

Practise reading passages quickly and see how much you can remember – the more you do it, the easier it gets.

WHY START A READING CLUB?

A reading club makes reading more fun – you get to meet up with your friends, review books for each other and discuss what you have read. Did you enjoy the *Harry Potter* books? Or the *Dark Materials* trilogy by Philip Pullman? Then form your own reading club and talk about them!

The other benefit of such a club is that everyone's reading improves, of course!

START A READING CLUB!

HOW DO I GET STARTED?

First, form your group. You should aim for four to five people, including you. Ask your friends at home and at school.

Choose a name for your club – let everyone have a vote!

Design a logo or badge to show what your club is about and make some badges.

Decide how often you will meet.

Make some membership cards.

Mel
Bookworm Gang

Reading Club

Bookworm Gang

Name _____

Card No. _____

Signature _____

★ ★ ★ ★
★ **top tip** ★
Make posters for your club.
You could use pictures cut
from magazines to
illustrate them.

YOUR CLUB'S ACTIVITIES

What activities can your club do?

✦ Review books.

✦ Make up plays using stories you have read.

✦ Keep reading journals and diaries.

✦ Write and make books for younger children.

✦ Keep a scrapbook of book reviews found in newspapers and magazines.

✦ Make your own reading club Web page where other people can read your reviews.

Let's start our own reading club!

Wouldn't a cake club be better?

TEST ROUND-UP

COMPREHENSION TEST

Read the passages below, then answer the questions.

Remember:

● Skim-read the text

● Read the questions and find the key words

● Scan the text for the answers.

SECTION ONE

THE LEGEND OF ZELDA – THE OCARINA OF TIME

This game is full of exciting and imaginative characters and adventures. Link, the hero, tries to stop Ganondorf, the evil wizard, from collecting three magical gems: the Kokiri Emerald, the Goron Ruby and the Zora Sapphire. These jewels, along with the Ocarina of Time and the Sacred Sword, allow the holder to enter the Sacred Realm.

Ganondorf wants to enter the Sacred Realm to take control of the Tri force, the source of ultimate power. The Tri force is made up of three elements: Power, Wisdom and Bravery. If someone evil tries to take control of the Tri force, it will split into three parts. Ganondorf will take Power and will be able to corrupt the world.

QUESTIONS
1. What is the hero of *The Legend of Zelda* called?
2. Who is Ganondorf?
3. Why does Ganondorf want to enter the Sacred Realm?
4. What is the Tri force made up from?
5. What happens if an evil person takes control of the Tri force?

SECTION TWO

THE BLACK DEATH

The Black Death, a terrible plague, reached England in 1348. It spread from the port of Weymouth to Bristol and, in spite of closing the roads, quickly spread to Gloucester. It then passed to Oxford and from there to London. By the spring it was at its height. It seemed to attack men rather than women, and the young and strong rather than the elderly.

The plague continued to ravage Europe for centuries. The Tudor period saw repeated plagues. People carried sponges soaked in vinegar and posies of flowers, called tussie-mussies, to ward off the plague fumes. They did not realise that the plague was carried by the fleas on the rats they saw everywhere.

The nursery rhyme 'Ring-a-ring-o' roses' dates from the time of the plague:

Ring-a-ring-o' roses,   (The rash, that came with the plague, appeared in red rings on the skin.)

A pocket full of posies,   (The tussie-mussies that people carried to ward off the plague.)

Ah-tishoo! Ah-tishoo!   (Sneezing – a symptom of the plague.)

We all fall down.   (Everyone dies.)

QUESTIONS

1. When did the plague reach England?
2. Who seemed most likely to be infected by the plague?
3. How did people try to avoid the plague?
4. What was the plague really caused by?
5. What does the line 'Ah-tishoo! Ah-tishoo! We all fall down' refer to?

So Ring-a-roses is about the plague?

And I thought it was just a sweet, little kid's rhyme!

★ **top tip** ★

Remember to read the passages through carefully so you don't make any silly mistakes!

CONFUSING CLAUSES

WHAT IS A CLAUSE?

A <u>clause</u> is a part of a sentence. It has a subject and a verb. It is not a sentence, so it does not have to start with a capital letter or end with a full stop.

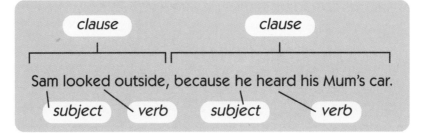

A <u>simple sentence</u> has one clause.

COMPOUND SENTENCES

<u>Compound sentences</u> have two important clauses. Each clause would make a simple sentence on its own, but can be joined to make a compound sentence. Words such as 'and', 'because' and 'so' are used to join the clauses to make a compound sentence.

She jumped in the air. She was excited.

She jumped in the air, because she was excited.

Each clause makes sense on its own and each clause is as important as the other.

★ **top tip** ★
Remember, a clause has a subject and a verb.

38

COMPLEX SENTENCES

A complex sentence is built around a <u>main clause</u> and also has less important clauses. The main clause is the most important part of the sentence and contains the main idea. It would make sense on its own.

The less important clauses are called <u>subordinate clauses</u>.

main clause	subordinate clause

Helen ran quickly, because she saw the ice cream van.

I'm really complex – does that make me important?

No, Sam – you're just a subordinate ...

QUICK TEST

1. What is a simple sentence?

2. What is a clause?

3. What is a complex sentence?

HAVE A GO ...

When you are reading, try to work out if sentences are simple, compound or complex.

ANSWERS: 1. A single clause with a subject and a verb.
2. A statement with a subject and a verb.
3. A statement with more than one clause.

39

CONTRACTIONS

WHAT ARE CONTRACTIONS?

Contractions are words that have letters missing. An apostrophe shows where the letters have been missed out. Words like this are used in informal writing, such as:

- Letters to friends

- When a character in a story is speaking

- Contractions are not used in pieces of formal writing, such as reports or formal letters.

Isn't a contraction where something gets smaller?

I thought it was a funny machine – oh no, that's a contraption!

CONTRACTIONS

These are examples of contractions:

I cannot → I can't

I am → I'm

I have → I've

We are → we're

Does not → doesn't

I had → I'd

I would → I'd

They are → they're

He will → he'll

She will → she'll

Who is → who's

Shall not → shan't

Will not → won't

You have → you've

won't!

★ top tip ★

Remember, do not use contractions in formal writing.

QUICK TEST

Change these words to their contracted form:

1. Will not

2. Can not

3. You have

4. They are

5. Do not

6. She will

HAVE A GO ...

Write a sentence with lots of contractions and see how fast you can read it.

ANSWERS: **1.** Won't **2.** Can't **3.** You've **4.** They're **5.** Don't **6.** She'll

IT'S MINE!

POSSESSIVE APOSTROPHES

Apostrophes can be used to show that something belongs to somebody.

They are called <u>possessive apostrophes</u>.

To show something belongs to somebody, we add an apostrophe followed by an s.

The bowl that belongs to the cat ➜ the cat's bowl.

The drink that belongs to the girl ➜ the girl's drink.

The book that belongs to the boy ➜ the boy's book.

POSSESSIVES ENDING IN 'S'

What happens when a word already ends in s?

When a word already ends in s, the apostrophe is sometimes added without adding another s.

> The sister belonging to James → James' sister

But other times, another s is added.

> The hospital established by St Thomas → St Thomas's Hospital

Sam's very possessive about his scooter!

★ top tip ★

When the word ending in 's' is a group of people, an apostrophe is added without an 's.'

The gardens belonging to our neighbours → our neighbours' gardens.

But Mel's even more possessive about her sweets!

QUICK TEST

Add the possessive apostrophes to these sentences:

1. The cats fur was matted.

2. The girls eyes were blue.

3. The dogs collar was red.

ANSWERS: 1. cat's 2. girl's 3. dog's

HAVE A GO ...

Read a newspaper article and look out for all the words with possessive apostrophes.

43

PUNCTUATION

Punctuation helps to make writing *make sense*.
Without punctuation, passages would just be a *collection of words*.

Read this passage:

> The dog ran around the garden chasing hens it was brown and the hens were white yesterday the dog dug up lots of flowers in the flowerbed

It *doesn't make much sense*, does it?

Read it again, *with the punctuation*:

> The dog ran around the garden, chasing hens. It was brown and the hens were white. Yesterday, the dog dug up lots of flowers in the flowerbed.

It makes more sense *with punctuation!*

PERFECT PUNCTUATION!

ENDING SENTENCES

Full stops are put at the *end of a sentence* to show it has finished. *Question marks* go at the end of a sentence when it is a *question*. *Exclamation marks* are used at the *end of a sentence*, which shows surprise or fear – any *exclamation*. Exclamations are used to show someone is shouting. You use a question mark or an *exclamation mark* instead of a full stop. When you start a new sentence, you use a *capital letter*.

Is that my coat?

That's my coat!

COMMAS

Commas are used to divide different parts of a sentence. Commas help to make things clear.

Commas separate <u>main clauses</u> from <u>dependent clauses</u> in <u>complex sentences</u>. (see pages 38–39)

Without a comma:

> When the play was over the people went home.

With a comma:

> When the play was over, the people went home.

The meaning is made clear with the use of a comma. In the first sentence, it sounds as though the play was above the people!

★ **top tip** ★

Always read your work back to yourself to make sure you have used the correct punctuation and that your work makes sense.

I LIKE EXCLAMATION MARKS, BECAUSE I LIKE SHOUTING!

You would!

QUICK TEST

1. What are commas used for?

2. When are exclamation marks used?

3. Which of these sentences should end with a question mark?

   a. He asked me why I read that book

   b. Why did you read that book

HAVE A GO ...

Re-write a passage from a book you are reading without punctuation. Does it make sense or does it mean something different?

ANSWERS: **1.** They are used to divide sentences. **2.** At the end of sentences, instead of a question mark or full stop. **3.** b.

LET'S TALK ABOUT IT!

REPORTED SPEECH

<u>Reported speech</u> means someone is telling the reader about something somebody else has said.

Then he said he was going home.

The man shouted hello as he came into the room.

The teacher told us all to put our hands up.

Reported speech does not use speech marks.

This doesn't mean you can just repeat exactly the words a person says.

For example:
If your Mum said, "Don't be rude to my sister," you might report it as:
Mum told us not to upset Auntie.

SPEECH MARKS

Speech marks are used when someone is actually speaking.

> "I'm going home!" said the man.

When somebody starts to speak, the words inside speech marks always start with a capital letter, even if they are not at the beginning of a sentence.

> Then the girl said, "I like cats, even if they have fleas!"

Speech marks always end with a punctuation mark inside the speech marks. If someone is surprised or shouting, use an exclamation mark. If it is a question, use a question mark.

"I like cats, even if they have fleas!"

★ top tip ★

Remember – speech marks are only used when someone is actually speaking.

Blah, blah, blah, blah

If Sam was a character in a story, you'd have to use loads of speech marks! He never stops talking!

QUICK TEST

Add speech marks where necessary to these sentences:

1. The boy said that he hated mashed potato.

2. I like science fiction films best, said Melanie.

3. Would you like a sweet? asked Bethany.

ANSWERS: 1. Reported speech – no speech marks. 2. "I like science fiction films best," said Melanie. 3. "Would you like a sweet?" asked Bethany.

HAVE A GO ...

Make a list of all the different words you can use instead of said. Asked, laughed, exclaimed ... it will make your work much more interesting!

PLURALS

When you are writing or talking about *more than one thing*, it is called a <u>plural</u>. Usually, you just write a word and *add an 's' to the end* to make it a plural:

cat → cats	bird → birds
flower → flowers	chair → chairs

But there are some words that are a *bit trickier*!

If a word already ends in s, you *cannot add another s*! Instead, you add *es*.

dress → dresses	mess → messes
press → presses	

PUZZLING PLURALS

WORDS ENDING IN -Y

Words that *end in y* have *special rules* – but it's still confusing!

Most words that *end in y* lose the *y* and add *ies*:

lady → ladies	pony → ponies
baby → babies	puppy → puppies

But there are some *exceptions*!

donkey → donkeys

Just to confuse you!

★ top tip ★

Learn tricky plurals by writing the single version of the word on one side of a piece of paper and the plural on the other side – then test yourself.

WORDS ENDING IN -F

When words ending in *f* change from single to plural, the *f* almost always changes to *ves*.

leaf ➜ leaves   hoof ➜ hooves

calf ➜ calves   dwarf ➜ dwarves

WORDS ENDING IN -O

When words ending in *o* change from single to plural, there is a special rule:

o adds *es*

tomato ➜ tomatoes   potato ➜ potatoes

But – you guessed – there are exceptions!

piano ➜ pianos

So would the plural of Sam be Sams?

Yuk, I can't cope with you being anything other than singular!

QUICK TEST

Change these words from singular to plural:

1. Dog

2. Piano

3. Calf

4. Baby

HAVE A GO ...

Some words have strange plurals – and you just have to learn them!

- mouse ➜ mice
- house ➜ houses
- child ➜ children
- goose ➜ geese.

ANSWERS: **1.** Dogs **2.** Pianos **3.** Calves **4.** Babies

CONFUSING WORDS

Some words can be confusing – it is *easy to make mistakes* about where to use:

✦ there and their ✦ of and off ✦ to, too and two

These sets of words *sound the same*, but *mean different things*. They are also spelled differently. Words like this are called <u>homophones</u>.

WEIRD WORDS!

THERE AND THEIR

There is used when you are writing about place.

> My coat is over there. There she is!

Their is used to show belonging.

> That dog is theirs. Their favourite game is football.

OF AND OFF

Off is used to mean a change in position:

> He jumped off the pier into the water.

It is also used in other ways:

> The boy was afraid he would be told off for being cheeky.
> The dog ran off down the lane.

Of is used to show belonging:

> The days of the week. A group of children.

TO, TWO AND TOO

Two is a number:

Two cats were fighting.

Too can mean 'as well':

I want to come too.

It can also be used to mean having more than you want of something:

That's too much cake!
I'm too hot.

To can mean direction:

I'm going to the shops.

And also to express an action:

I want to buy some chocolate, please.
I want to see the crown jewels.

Mel asked if I wanted to eat a cake too.

But Sam said I was greedy – so I ate two!

★ top tip ★
Try to learn the differences between these words and when they are used – they are common mistakes!

QUICK TEST

Choose the right word to fill the gaps, looking at the above examples to help you:

1. I went to/too/two the shops.

2. I fell off/of the chair!

3. They asked for there/their pocket money.

ANSWERS: 1. to 2. off 3. their

HAVE A GO ...

Can you think of any other pairs or groups of words that sound the same, but mean something different? For example:
Pair/pear/pare

USEFUL WORDS

There are some words you are expected to know as a part of your work in the Literacy Hour at school. You need to make sure you can use them.

* Vowel   * Consonant   * Syllable

TRICKY TERMINOLOGY!

VOWELS

<u>Vowels</u> are the letters a, e, i, o, u. In the English language, every word has to have at least *one vowel* – and that is where a complication comes in: the letter y can also act as a vowel!

| Try | My |
| Fry | Spy |

Can you think of any other words where y acts as a vowel?

A <u>consonant</u> is any letter of the alphabet that is *not a vowel*.

SYLLABLES

Syllables are chunks of sound that you hear in a word as you say it.

The word dog has one syllable.

The word rabbit has two syllables.
rabb – it

The word butterfly has three syllables.
butt – er – fly

The word alligator has four syllables.
al – li – ga – tor

How many syllables are there in your name?

There is one syllable in my name: Sam.

And there is one in mine: Mel.

★ **top tip** ★

A good way to count syllables is to clap them as you say words.

QUICK TEST

Try clapping these words and count the syllables.

1. Aeroplane

2. Calamity

3. Motorway

4. Guitar

ANSWERS: 1. 3 2. 4 3. 3 4. 2

HAVE A GO ...

How many vowels are there in your name?

WHAT DO WE MEAN BY NOUNS?

A <u>noun</u> is a *naming word*. It may be a thing, a person or a place.

There are three types of nouns you need to know about and identify:

Common nouns **Proper nouns** **Collective nouns**

KNOW YOUR NOUNS!

COMMON NOUNS

Common nouns are the general names of things.

Dog, cat, cow, horse – *common nouns*.

Boy, girl, man, woman – *common nouns*.

Table, chair, television, computer – *common nouns*.

PROPER NOUNS

Proper nouns are the names of particular people, places or things. They have a capital letter.

Bethany, Luke, Durham, Brighton – *proper nouns*.

COLLECTIVE NOUNS

Collective nouns name groups of things.

They have special names for different groups, but some of the most common include:
Army of soldiers
Herd of cows
Flock of seagulls

So, a bunch of bananas is a collective noun?

No, it's a monkey's breakfast!

QUICK TEST

Are these proper, collective or common nouns?

1. Newcastle Upon Tyne

2. Cat

3. Family

ANSWERS: 1. Proper 2. Common 3. Collective

HAVE A GO ...

Can you think of any other collective nouns? See if you can find any in today's newspaper.

WHAT ARE VERBS?

<u>Verbs</u> are the words that describe actions. Every sentence has to have a verb or it is not a sentence! Verbs tell you what a person or thing is doing.

The girl is jumping.
The word jumping is the verb.

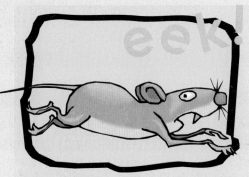

The mouse squeaked.
The word squeaked is the verb.

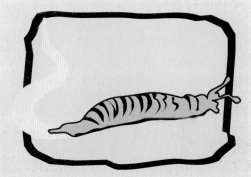

The slug slithered.
The word slithered is the verb.

The boy is playing football.
The word playing is the verb.

VITAL VERBS

PASSIVE VERBS

Passive verbs tell you about what is being done. A sentence with a passive verb tells you about the thing or person that the action is happening to. It does not always say what or who is doing the action, though!

The table was polished.

ACTIVE VERBS

Active verbs **tell you** what is being done **by someone or something.**

> Marie polished the table.
>
> Grendal growled at the mouse.

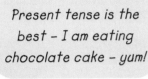 *Present tense is the best – I am eating chocolate cake – yum!*

You're too greedy to ever need future tense!

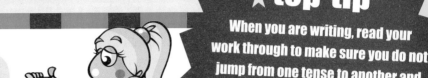 ★ **top tip** ★

When you are writing, read your work through to make sure you do not jump from one tense to another and back again. Sometimes, teachers read stories that sound like they have taken place in a time machine because of all the flipping backwards and forwards!

TENSES

Verbs change <u>tense</u> to show us **when things happen:** past, present (now) and future.

> I ate the chocolate ice cream – *past*.
>
> I am eating the chocolate cake – *present* (now).
>
> I shall eat the chocolate ice cream – *future*.

QUICK TEST

Active (A) or passive (P)?

1. The cat was stroked.

2. The squirrel jumped.

3. The door was opened.

HAVE A GO …

When you are reading, see if you can identify whether verbs are active or passive.

ANSWERS: 1. Passive 2. Active 3. Passive

57

ADDING ADJECTIVES

WHAT ARE ADJECTIVES?

<u>Adjectives</u> are *describing* words. They describe a <u>noun</u> in a sentence.

The *huge* squid slithered into the *dark* cave.

Huge is the adjective that describes squid, and *dark* is the adjective that describes cave.

The *stinking* rubbish was rotting on the *enormous* tip.

Stinking is the adjective that describes rubbish, and *enormous* is the adjective that describes tip.

The *glittering* snow sparkled like *white* sugar.

Glittering is the adjective that describes snow, and *white* is the adjective that describes sugar.

MAKING YOUR WRITING EXCITING

Adjectives are a powerful tool for a writer. They are describing words and descriptions are what make people want to read more. Adjectives can help to make vivid word pictures in the mind of your reader.

Compare these sentences:

- The snail slithered across the path.

- The delicate, pink snail slithered across the mossy, tiled path.

Which sentence makes the best word picture? The sentence with adjectives, of course!

- The poppy petals blew away on the wind.

- The scarlet, silken poppy petals blew away on the warm wind.

Which sentence makes the best word picture? Once again, the sentence with adjectives.

I like vivid descriptions – annoying, noisy, clumsy – that just about describes Sam!

At least I'm not a boring, bossy bookworm!

★ **top tip** ★

Make a note of your favourite, most descriptive adjectives when you are reading, and try to use them in your own work.

QUICK TEST

Add adjectives to these sentences to make them more interesting:

1. The rabbit was eating a lettuce leaf.

2. The ghost walked through a wall.

3. The cake was on the plate.

HAVE A GO ...

Can you find adjectives when you are reading? Is a book more interesting if it uses lots of adjectives?

ANSWERS: Suggestions only **1.** Fluffy, juicy. **2.** Terrifying, crumbling. **3.** Delicious, yellow.

AGILE ADVERBS

WHAT ARE ADVERBS?

Adverbs are words that describe verbs.

The fox ran quickly.

The word quickly is the adverb. It describes the verb ran, telling us how it was done.

The woman chuckled quietly.

The word quietly is the adverb. It describes the verb chuckled, telling us how it was done.

The rat crept slowly into the barn.

The word slowly is the adverb. It describes the verb crept, telling us how it was done.

★ top tip ★

Adverbs are another way of making your writing more interesting, as they add to your descriptive word pictures – so make sure you use them!

VERSATILE ADVERBS!

Adverbs are words like completely, totally, quite and very. Adverbs are used with adjectives. The adverb shows how much of the adjective describes the noun.

The woman was very beautiful.

The dog was quite scruffy.

The cake was completely ruined.

I'm the fastest runner in my class!

You have a very vivid imagination!

QUICK TEST

Underline the adverbs:

1. The boy walked slowly.

2. The dog was very noisy.

3. The woman ran quickly.

ANSWERS: 1. Slowly 2. Very 3. Quickly

HAVE A GO ...

Read an article in a magazine or newspaper and underline all the adverbs you can find.

61

WHAT IS A PRONOUN?

<u>Pronouns</u> do the same job as <u>nouns</u>. Words like *he, she, it, mine* and *yours* are all pronouns. They are used in the place of nouns. They are very useful, because they stop you from repeating yourself. If your writing was full of the same words being repeated, it could easily become dull.

Read this passage:

> Kevin picked up his bag and then Kevin looked inside. Kevin was worried, because Kevin thought the book was missing. Kevin searched for the book.

The passage has a lot of Kevins, doesn't it? You could use *he* and *his* instead of Kevin.

> Kevin picked up his bag and then he looked inside. He was worried, because he thought the book was missing. He searched for it.

Pronouns make writing flow more *naturally*.

PERPLEXING PRONOUNS

USEFUL PRONOUNS

Read this list of pronouns. They are really useful words. You will already be using these words without realising that they are pronouns!

he	yours	they	them
she	I	me	us
it	you	him	
mine	we	her	

The only new thing you need to learn is that these common words are called pronouns.

A WORD OF CAUTION!

'They' and 'them' are easy to mix up and so are 'me' and 'my'. Have you ever heard anyone say, "Them are nice!"? People sometimes talk like that when speaking to friends, but it should never be written down in that way! The proper word to use would be 'they'. Read these sentences, where 'them' and 'they' have been mixed up.

"Them are rotten!" said Shelley. "I thought them were coming to meet us, but them never turned up! I thought them were me mates!"

Re-written, the sentence reads:

"They are rotten!" said Shelley. "I thought they were coming to meet us, but they never turned up! I thought they were my mates!"

I use lots of pronouns. I call Mel 'it' for example!

★ top tip ★

Make sure you use pronouns in your own writing – don't just keep repeating yourself!

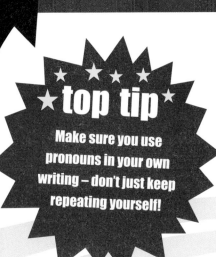

So I'm an 'It' girl!

QUICK TEST

Change the underlined words to pronouns to make the sentences sound better.

1. Ellie sat in the sandpit. <u>Ellie</u> liked the <u>sandpit</u>. <u>The sandpit</u> was <u>Ellie's</u> favourite toy.

2. The hedgehog was looking for slugs. <u>The hedgehog</u> was hungry.

3. John chased the horse. <u>The horse</u> had run away from <u>John</u> on the lane. <u>The horse</u> was making <u>John</u> cross.

HAVE A GO ...

Try to learn the word pronoun. Remember which words are pronouns.

ANSWERS: 1. She liked it. It was her favourite toy. **2.** It was hungry **3.** It had run away from him on the lane. It was making him cross.

PLACING PREPOSITIONS

WHAT ARE PREPOSITIONS?

Prepositions are words that tell you the answer to the questions where and when.

Prepositions tell you the relation between pronouns (see page 62) and nouns (see page 54).

The spider is under the bed. (Where)

The girl climbed into the huge box. (Where)

I jumped on to the bus just in time! (Where)

There are all sorts of treasures between these cushions! (Where)

There it is, in front of you! (Where)

Let's do our homework after we've been to the youth club. (When)

Then she said, "You can't have a cake until you've eaten those spinach patties." (When)

The underlined words are all prepositions.

WHAT ARE CONJUNCTIONS?

Conjunctions are joining words. They are used to join other words and clauses (see page 38).

And, but, also and because are all conjunctions.

Compare these sentences:

> The fly buzzed. It was cross.
>
> The fly buzzed, because it was cross.

> The goat liked dock leaves. It didn't like dandelions.
>
> The goat liked dock leaves, but it didn't like dandelions.

> The girl liked chips. She liked bean burgers.
>
> The girl liked chips and she liked bean burgers.

top tip

Conjunctions are another type of word, like pronouns, that make your writing flow. When you are writing, read your work back. Would more conjunctions or prepositions make your work more interesting?

That's funny – I use sticky tape for joining things – not conjunctions!

Very funny ... not!

QUICK TEST

Underline the prepositions in these sentences:

1. I found a sticky lolly behind the cushion!

2. The mouse hid under the chair.

3. The dinosaur trod on the horsetails, squashing them flat.

ANSWERS: 1. Behind 2. Under 3. On

HAVE A GO ...

Make a conjunctions collection in a notebook. How many can you collect?

65

KEEP YOUR HAIR ON!

CLICHES

Cliches are words and phrases that have been used so many times that people get over-familiar – and bored – with them!

Cliches are often metaphors (see page 23):

As fresh as a daisy

When all is said and done …

At the end of the day …

It's raining cats and dogs!

These are all cliches – avoid them when you are writing! Cliches are a sort of idiom.

Starting on a level playing field, I would say that at the end of the day, you use more cliches than me, Mel.

You sound like a sports commentator!

IDIOMS

Idioms are common phrases that are used and understood – but should not be taken literally!

You really take the biscuit!

It doesn't mean you are a biscuit burglar – but that you are the absolute limit!

I'm feeling a bit under the weather today.

It doesn't mean you are being squashed by a cloud, or in fact anything to do with rain, sun etc.! It means you are feeling a bit poorly.

Keep your hair on!

It doesn't mean 'don't go bald' – it means 'don't be cross'!

The funny thing about idioms is that they are different in different places and countries. One of the hardest things for people to learn, when they are studying a foreign language, is the idioms that people who speak the language as their mother tongue grow up with and understand.

Did you know ...

In Denmark, if you stayed indoors all the time, you would be called a *stueplante* – a houseplant!

A Danish bookworm is called a *læsehest* – a reading horse!

'No cow on the ice' means 'no problem', and if people think you are a bit potty, they say you have 'rats in the attic' – a bit like our English idiom, 'bats in the belfry'.

You can't work out the meaning of an idiom just by looking at the everyday meaning of the words – you need to know them – and if not, you need to learn!

★ **top tip** ★
Remember – idioms are not supposed to be taken literally!

QUICK TEST

What do these idioms mean?

1. She wraps her grandad around her little finger!

2. He's very confusing – he's always blowing hot and cold.

ANSWERS: 1. Her grandad lets her have her way. **2.** He likes things one minute and not the next.

HAVE A GO ...

Listen when people are talking – can you spot the idioms?

WHY IS SPELLING SO HARD?

English is a *funny language*. It is made up of words from so *many different cultures and languages* – Anglo Saxon, Norman French, Latin, Celtic – that it is hard to understand all the *different spellings* you encounter! Perhaps so many *different languages* have given us words because we live on an island. We have had lots of visitors – and conquerors – over thousands of years.

There are a few *spelling rules* that can help you to remember how to spell words – but it's still *hard work!*

RULES, RULES...!

GENERAL SPELLING RULES

* *'I' before the 'e' except after 'c'* – like in 'receive.' But be careful – it's only a general rule and doesn't always work.

* *If a word ends in a silent 'e', lose the 'e' before you add the suffixes '-ed' or '-ing.'*

  > *decide* **becomes** *decided* **and** *deciding*

* When a one-<u>syllable</u> word adds a suffix beginning with a <u>vowel</u>, you should double the last <u>consonant</u>.

  > trap → trapping
  >
  > hit → hitting

* When you add *full, till, well* and *all* to words, either as <u>prefixes</u> or <u>suffixes</u>, you always lose one of the 'l's.

  > help + full = helpful
  >
  > all + ways = always

SILLY SENTENCES AND WORDS WITHIN WORDS

You can make up silly sentences to help you to learn spellings that you find difficult. A really useful one is, 'There is a rat in separate.'

You can also look for words within words – such as the in their, cot + age in cottage. Breaking down words into these smaller words makes them easier to spell.

★ **top tip** ★

Don't forget the old way of learning spellings – look (look at the word), write (write the word) cover (cover it up), check (see if it is right) – it works!

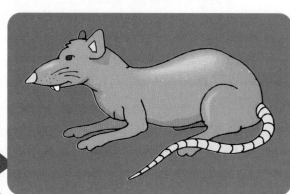

You can find Mel in smell!

Well, your feet smell like balsamic vinegar!

HAVE A GO ...

Choose a short word, such as cat. See how many longer words you can find with the word cat hidden inside.

- CATerpillar
- CATamaran
- CATastrophe
- DeliCATe ...

QUICK TEST

Can you find any words within words in this list?

1. musically
2. tomato
3. carriage

ANSWERS: **1.** Music, us, call, ally **2.** Tom, mat, to, at **3.** Car, age

69

THINK THESAURUS!

EXCITING VOCABULARY

Each piece of writing is only as exciting as the words or vocabulary that you, as the author, decide to use. That is true whether you are writing a story, a poem or a piece of non-fiction.

You should constantly be looking out for new and exciting words – words that you hear on the television or radio, or words that you read in books, papers or magazines.

You could keep a notebook, not arranged alphabetically, but in subjects, i.e. words you would associate with ghost stories, seashore words, jungle words, space words – whatever it is that you find interesting.

For example: Ghost words
- lonely
- ghastly
- transparent
- gloom
- creaking
- soft breeze

BUILD YOUR OWN THESAURUS!

A *thesaurus* is a book that gives the reader *lots of different ways of saying the same word.* It helps writers to avoid their work becoming repetitive and boring.

Look at these lists:

Not just *small* but: minute   minuscule   microscopic   diminutive

Not just *big* but: gigantic   titanic   vast   gargantuan

Not just *sad* but: desolate   dejected   gloomy   miserable

Can you add any other words?

And can you make lists for these words:

Cold, hot, noisy ... and any others you may want to use!

★ **top tip** ★

When you are collecting vocabulary, look for unusual words that you have not seen before, but would like to use. Don't be afraid to borrow words and phrases that you find. But do not just copy descriptions word-for-word. Change them and make them your own.

I am so desolate! A curtain of grey water, like shards of glass, is pounding on the windowpane ...

I think she's fed up because it's raining...!

QUICK TEST

Can you think of other ways to say:

1. said

2. walk

3. eat

ANSWERS: **1.** Shout, call, reply, whisper ...
2. Stride, step, saunter, march ...
3. Gobble, taste, consume, munch ...

HAVE A GO ...

Don't forget to collect interesting onomatopoeic words for your thesaurus, too! (see page 24)

MAKING MOODS

CREATING MOODS

When you read a passage in your Year Six SATs exam (National Test), you may be asked how the author has used language to create a particular mood or feeling.

Read this passage. It was written by a boy in Year Six, who had been studying *Romeo and Juliet*. He is retelling the story of Scene One.

As you read, try to think about how he has used language to create the right mood for the piece.

> The families meet in the street and animosity flares.
>
> 'Are you insulting us?' asked a Capulet of a nearby group of jeering Montagues.
>
> 'I do insult,' the young man sneered.
>
> 'But do you insult us?' a Capulet questioned.
>
> 'Raise your swords and drown the Capulets in their own blood!' bellowed a Montague.
>
> The Capulets rushed the Montagues, swinging their swords, and the Montagues parried their blows. Blood flew from wounds inflicted by biting blades. Screams of anguish and victorious yells echoed through the surrounding alleys. Blood trickled thickly among the cobbles.

top tip

Read different genres of story and see if you can work out how the author sets the scene and builds atmosphere – then use the same strategies in your own stories!

HOW DID HE DO IT?

The passage is very effective and the boy got a good mark for the piece of work that the passage is taken from. The passage is about the way that the two families, the Montagues and the Capulets, fight and the hatred they feel for one another.

The passage uses interesting vocabulary such as 'animosity', 'jeered' and 'sneered'. They sound right for the Shakespearian subject being discussed. He uses alliteration (see page 25) to describe the action 'biting blades' – which sounds like a sword cutting flesh.

'Screams of anguish and victorious yells' is much more interesting than using words such as 'shouting' – the writer has thought about using varied and interesting vocabulary.

'Blood trickled thickly among the cobbles' makes a vivid – but horrific – picture in the reader's mind's eye and this helps to build the idea that the play is going to be violent and bloody – which it is!

I like biting blades – nearly as cool as my sizzling scooter!

Sluggish scooter more like!

QUICK TEST

Which words or phrases do you feel build the mood of suspense and brewing violence?

HAVE A GO ...

When you are reading a story, think about the way the author builds the mood. If it is a suspense story, for example, the author may have used very short sentences to add tension to the story.

73

PARAGRAPHS

Paragraphs are used to organise writing into sections, so that the writing makes sense. New paragraphs are used to introduce new ideas. Each paragraph generally has its own topic, but that does not mean that the ideas in the following paragraphs do not have links.

Leaving a line between paragraphs (a bit like we just have here!) shows clearly that a new paragraph has started.

If you do not break your work into paragraphs, it makes it much harder to understand.

★ top tip ★

In your own writing, remember that each paragraph should have an idea of its own.

PUNCHY PARAGRAPHS

ONE BIG LUMP!

Read this passage – it has been written without using paragraphs:

The girl slouched as she leaned against the wall. She was bored. It was the first day of the summer holidays and practically everyone she knew was already away on holiday. Not her, though. And there would be no holiday this year. Not a real one, anyway. She was going along to a conference with her Mum for two weeks – which her Mum had promised would be "great fun" – but that wasn't how Charlotte saw it. Some fancy hotel where she'd be dumped all day again. What fun was it being able to access cable and room service if there was no one to share it with. It hadn't always been that way, though. Charlotte remembered other holidays, other years – when they were another family. That was before her dad had left. They'd had holidays at the beach, rented a house in the woods and by the lake … but now he'd gone. Charlotte felt a bit left out now he had a new family. She knew he loved her and everything, but when she visited, he and his new wife Suki (and what sort of name was that anyway for a grown woman?) spent all their time running after the baby.

NEW PARAGRAPHS

How do you know when to start a new paragraph?

This is the passage you have already read, but this time it has been broken up into short paragraphs. If you read books for teenagers, you will find that the paragraphs are often really quite short, like this:

> The girl slouched as she leaned against the wall. She was bored. It was the first day of the summer holidays, and practically everyone she knew was already away on holiday.
>
> Not her, though. And there would be no holiday this year. Not a real one, anyway. She was going along to a conference with her Mum for two weeks – which her Mum had promised would be "great fun" – but that wasn't how Charlotte saw it. Some fancy hotel where she'd be dumped all day again. What fun was it being able to access cable and room service, if there was no one to share it with?
>
> It hadn't always been that way, though. Charlotte remembered other holidays, other years – when they were another family. That was before her dad had left. They'd had holidays at the beach, rented a house in the woods and by the lake … but now he'd gone.
>
> Charlotte felt a bit left out, now he had a new family. She knew he loved her and everything, but when she visited, he and his new wife Suki (and what sort of name was that anyway for a grown woman?) spent all their time running after the baby.

New ideas?

Yes, Sam – a bit of a radical concept for you!

QUICK TEST

1. Why do you think the passage has been broken up into the paragraphs in this way?

2. Why has each new paragraph been started?

ANSWERS: 1. So that each paragraph contains an idea of its own. 2. When the train of thought turns to a new idea.

HAVE A GO …

Next time you read a novel, check the paragraphs – why has each paragraph been started? Does it mark an easy-to-identify new idea?

GETTING STARTED ...

STORY STARTERS

What makes you want to read a story? Once you have got past the cover and possibly read the <u>blurb</u> on the back, it is the opening sentences that hook you and make you want to read more.

Read these story starters:

> The girl huddled into the damp corner of the alley, pressing herself back into the darkness. Her breath came in sobs – what if they heard her?

> "Come back here, boy!" boomed the angry voice. The scruffy boy scrabbled out through the doorway into the sunshine. Parcels of food crammed his bulging pockets. His family was starving and he, as the man of the family now, was not about to let that happen.

> A tentacle uncoiled slowly, like a vast rubbery rope. It felt about delicately, probing rock crevices and holes for something to eat. Then it gently touched the toes of the boy, who felt a touch like a tiny crab scuttling across his feet.

Do they make you want to read more?

WRITING YOUR OWN STORIES

Think about the story starters you have just read. Did you like any of them? Each was written to make you wonder what happens next. In story one, what is chasing the girl? In the second story, why is the boy reduced to stealing? In the third story, will the boy get away? The story starters leave lots of questions hanging in the air, so that the reader wants to read on. That is what you have to do when you begin your own story.

STRATEGIES FOR STORY STARTERS

Here are some ideas to help you to *get started*.

- Start your stories with a *bang* – don't wander into the story with lots of details that can emerge as the story unfolds – *start the action straight away!*

- Make sure you introduce some sort of *question*, so the reader wants to *find out more*.

- Make sure that *right from the beginning* you use wonderful, *descriptive vocabulary*. It helps to *set the scene*.

- Concentrate hard on the beginning of your story – it is worth writing a couple of sentences in rough to make sure you can *re-draft* and change your work, making it as exciting as you can.

★ top tip ★

Read, read, read – then read some more! The more stories you read, the better your own stories will become, as you learn about different genres and styles of writing.

But Mum always says, 'Don't start telling me a story, now!'

I'm sure she wouldn't mind if you actually wrote some homework!

QUICK TEST

Choose one of these titles and write your own story starter.

- The Creature in the Darkness.

- Parent Trouble!

- I won't do THAT again!

- Friend or Foe?

HAVE A GO ...

Choose ten fiction books off the shelves – they could be from home, at school or in the library. Look at the first paragraph of each story. Do they all have a question that needs answering?

BRILLIANT BRAINSTORMS

BRAINSTORMING

When writers are going to *write a story*, they often have lots of *ideas* before they start. They often *make notes* to help them, perhaps in a notebook or more likely now on their computer!

One way to make notes is to do a <u>brainstorm</u>.

A *brainstorm* is just a *collection of ideas*, jotted down on paper. The ideas do not have to be written in *full sentences* – they can just be words or phrases written down as they come to you.

Look at this brainstorm of ideas for a story about a fire demon:

Useful words: sparks, licking flames, glittering, explosion

Girl thinks she sees him when a fire starts at her house

School /welfare services become involved

Parents begin to suspect she is setting fires herself – an arsonist?

Troublesome creature – tries to start fires maliciously

No one believes her – she sees the demon elsewhere – puts out fires in bins etc.

★ top tip ★

When you take your SATs at school, you will need to plan your story. Learning how to brainstorm will help you to get your ideas in order. It is a useful thing to do when writing non-fiction too, as it helps you think your ideas through really carefully.

GET LOTS OF PRACTICE

Try to do lots of brainstorms to get some practice. You can plan <u>non-fiction</u>, such as reports, in the same way. You could also write a brainstorm to plan an article for your school newsletter, if you have one. But planning stories is perhaps the best – because you can let your imagination *run wild*!

Here are some ideas for stories for you – write a brainstorm for these titles, and then choose your favourite and write the story!

The Dragon in the Cellar – you find a small dragon in the coal pile, which is getting smaller, because people don't believe in dragons any more.

Unwanted! Feral Cat Colony – life and battles amongst a colony of wild cats that no one wants, living on a rubbish tip in a big city.

My Brother's a Vampire! You make a really weird discovery one night. You knew your brother was mean, but ...!

Emergency at the Stables – a horse is injured and you are the only one who can get help!

My brain hurts!

All that brainstorming, I suppose – you're not used to thinking that hard!

HAVE A GO ...

Choose a fiction book that tells a really good story. If you had been the author, what important things from the story would have been in your brainstorm?

QUICK TEST

Write a brainstorm for a story about a new family that comes to live in your street. They only come out at night. They are all very pale indeed ...

WHAT A CHARACTER!

WHY ARE CHARACTERS IMPORTANT?

Think about the best stories you have ever read. What do you remember about them? Possibly some of the action, but mainly the characters!

Great characters:

* Pongwiffy the witch (in *Pongwiffy* by Kate Umansky) – mean, awful, dirty and funny!

* Aslan the lion (in *The Chronicles of Narnia* by C.S. Lewis) – noble, brave, loving and fierce.

* Hermione (in the *Harry Potter* books by J.K. Rowling) – brave, intelligent, good at solving problems.

* The Grand High Witch (in *The Witches* by Roald Dahl) – vicious, wicked and frightening.

* Amon the cat (in *The Cats of Seroster* by Robert Westall) – wise, courageous, loyal, 'faithful beyond death'.

Characters are the most important part of any story. If a character feels real, the reader will care about what happens to them – and will want to read more!

CHARACTER PROFILING

Sometimes, when teachers read stories, the characters are very thin – not much more than a name! In a really good story, characters are fleshed out and made real. Not an easy task!

That is where character profiling comes in. When you are planning a story, you need to really think about the characters – not just what they look like, but how they feel and how this affects their actions and motives.

Character profiling is drawing a picture in words of the person you are describing. To help you to write a profile, ask yourself these questions:

- What is the main reason for this character to appear in the story? If they have a task to do, perhaps you can make them strong-willed and full of purpose.

- If the character is a villain, do they have any redeeming features? (things that make them seem a little less wicked – love for a person or animal, or a reason in their past for why they act so badly).

- If the character is a hero, is there something they could do that is less than perfect – to make them a bit more human?

- How do they walk? Imagine being the character – how would they walk? Would they stride/creep/scuttle?

- How do they talk? Imagine the character saying something. Do they speak with confidence or are they shy?

Hmm, a profile of me: brave, bold, clever...!

Or daft, silly and vain...?

QUICK TEST

Write a character profile for:

1. A teenage girl in a mystery story.

2. A bully.

3. A very old, incredibly wise person.

HAVE A GO ...

After you have read a book, that you have really enjoyed, think about your favourite character. Could you write a profile for them?

81

HATCHING THE PLOT

PLANNING STORIES

It would be lovely, if everyone was so great at writing stories, that all they had to do was pick up a pen and let their creative genius flow. In the real world, though, we have to rely on things to help us along – like story plans. Story plans can be simple; some just ask you to think about the beginning, middle and end of your story. Others are more complicated and ask you to answer a series of questions.

Whichever type of story plan you use, it will help you to think about your story in detail before you start to write. In your KS2 <u>SATs</u>, you will be given a chance to quickly plan out your story. The more you know about story-planning in advance, the easier it will be – and you will get the best possible marks.

This page is as bad as my Mum asking all these questions!

Tell me about it...!

★ top tip ★

The more practice you get at writing story plans, the easier it will become – so practise!

QUESTIONS TO ASK YOURSELF

When you are planning a story, ask yourself these questions:

* Where does your story begin?

* Does the story setting help to build atmosphere? (If it is a ghost story, is the story set in a spooky place, for example.)

* Who is going to appear in your story? Do you have a main character? Are there any heroes or villains?

* Have you thought of a gripping beginning to hook your reader, so that they want to read more? (see page 77)

* How does the story develop? Are there any major changes or surprises during the story?

* Have you done a character profile? (see page 81)

* Have you thought of a good strong ending? Is there a twist in the tale (something unexpected at the end)?

QUICK TEST

Take the brainstorm you wrote for page 79 about the strange new family that have come to live in your street, and write a story plan using the questions above. You may even like to write the story!

HAVE A GO ...

Look at endings – how do writers make sure they write a good, strong ending? Short story collections are a good place to look.

BE A POET!

Poetry is a great source of descriptive and wonderful words. Look at th[e] examples below.

KENNINGS

<u>Kennings</u> are a way of describing things without actually saying what they are. A poem can be made by making a list of kennings.

Read this poem and try to guess what it is about!

Face-slapper
Finger-pincher
Frost-painter
Snow-bringer
Water-freezer
(*Winter*)

Now write your own kennings poem. You could make a booklet with your poem on one side and what it is about on the right-hand side under a flap, so people have to guess!

I'm going to write a kenning about Sam: sister-botherer, sweet-stealer ...

I'm going to write a kenning about football: crowd-thriller, scarf-flutterer ...

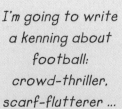

LIST POEMS

A list poem is just what it says – a list!
You could write a colour poem as a list.

Yellow is …
a ripe banana,
a juicy lemon,
the warmth of the sun.

Blue is …
the summer sea,
the sky at midday,
a robin's egg.

Green is …
a glistening tree frog,
a fresh spring leaf,
a grasshopper's wings.

Red is …
a glowing sunset,
a ladybird's back,
a silken poppy petal.

Now write your own list poem. You could write it about the seasons or
even the months of the year. You could write your lists on season shapes
(such as: spring – a lamb, summer – a sun,
autumn – a leaf, winter – a snowman) and
make a mobile for your room.

★ **top tip** ★

Try to read a variety of
poems – look for poetry
collections in the library
at school.

BE AN AUTHOR!

WRITING A STORY – THE WHOLE PROCESS!

You are going to test your skills as an author now – from brainstorm to final draft!

✦ Brainstorm

✦ Story plan

✦ Character profile

✦ Story starter

✦ Strong ending

Your choice of titles is:

✦ *The Voice in the Darkness*

✦ *October Story*

You can decide to make your story any genre you want – romance, science fiction, horror – you choose!

I'm doing The October Story about an annoying autumn ghoul on a skateboard that crashes into everyone and shouts a lot ...

STAGE ONE

BRAINSTORM – Remember to *jot down all of your ideas* and exciting vocabulary.

STORY PLAN – check page 83 to remind yourself of the *questions you need to ask*.

CHARACTER PROFILE – *make your characters real*, so the reader cares about what happens to them.

STAGE TWO

STORY STARTER – think of an exciting way to *hook your readers*, to make them want to find out more.

STORY ENDING – make sure your *story does not just fizzle out* – 'and then they had their tea/went to bed'. Make it interesting!

THE END

★ **top tip** ★
Read as many stories as you can – it is the best way to learn the craft of writing.

I'm doing The Voice In the Darkness – *a horror story about a terrifying being that creeps into my bedroom every night and gets in the bunk bed above me ...*

NATIONAL TEST PRACTICE

WRITING A STORY

You are going to write a story. By the time you take your SATs, you will be an expert!

You can decide to make your story any genre you want – romance, science fiction, horror – you choose!

Remember to follow these stages:

- Brainstorm – Remember to jot down all of your ideas and exciting vocabulary.

- Story plan – check pages 82–83 to remind yourself of the questions you need to ask.

- Character profile – make your characters lifelike, so the reader cares about what happens to them.

- Story ending – make sure your story does not just fizzle out – 'and then they had their tea/went to bed' … Make it exciting!

top tip

Don't forget to use exciting vocabulary whenever you can. Try to use some onomatopoeia (p.24) or other word effects if you can!

Choose from one of these story starters.

The mist swirled round her, like dead white fingers pulling at her ankles. She shuddered as she thought of the task that lay before her.

"What do you mean, stupid?" grumbled Macy. "I think after what you've just suggested, you're the stupid one!"

The sun glittered on the water, like millions of shards of glass. The boy stared out to sea, wondering how long he would have to wait.

The grey rain trickled down the car window. Gemma listened as the wipers swished rhythmically. She felt as miserable as the weather.

COMPREHENSION

Read the passage below, then answer the questions.

Chapter One

Eleanor dangled her suntanned arm out of the car window as her mother drove across the purple and green patchwork moors. She leaned her head against the headrest, closing her eyes. The sun was warming her skin, and she breathed in the spicy smell of the heather with a sigh of pleasure.

"Look, Eleanor!" Eleanor's mum Isobel pulled the car into a viewing point. She pointed to a dark shape gliding above the moor, its splayed wing feathers looking like fat brown fingers. "It's a buzzard! Do you know, for a long time, people thought that those magnificent birds killed lambs. So many were shot that they nearly died out. I read that the numbers were on the increase. What a grand sight!"

Her dark eyes sparkled. Eleanor smiled fondly at her mum. She loved the countryside and all the creatures in it. She started the engine up again, driving slowly and carefully on the winding road. They were on their way home. Eleanor's face glowed with excitement as she thought of the animals she would see that morning. She had been to visit her Godmother, Hilary and had missed all her pets. Eleanor adored Moss and Bramble, the sheepdogs, with their bright eyes that glittered with intelligence, and the way that the horses blew their warm musky breath on her hand as she gave them carrots.

As they pulled into the yard, they saw Eleanor's dad, Kevin. He looked a little anxious.

"Hi girls! Have a good time?" he asked. "Now, don't be worried, but Sweetpea has a nasty cut on her leg. The greedy thing escaped from her pen and was rooting about in the rubbish when she cut herself on a piece of broken glass. The cut is very deep, Isobel. I bathed it carefully in antiseptic, and covered the cut with a gauze pad. I'm not sure if she needs a vet."

"Oh, no! Let's take a look at her," said Isobel. The animals on the smallholding were mainly hers. She always worried about them when she was away from home. Eleanor scrambled out of the car and loped after her dad towards the goat shed. As they entered the shed, Eleanor was greeted by the warm, sweet smell of fresh hay wafting through the air. Sweetpea, an Angora goat, bleated pitifully and tried shakily to stand up. Isobel stroked the goat's soft, woolly flank and murmured soothingly to her. She examined the goat's leg quickly and efficiently, then turned to Eleanor.

"Could you fetch my first aid kit from the car, Eleanor?"

Eleanor slid off the straw bale she had chosen as a seat, the stalks tickling her legs as she moved. She scooted out of the door of the shed, running across the cobbled farmyard to the car. Soon she was back, clutching the kit.

"What a good helper you are," smiled Kevin. "I don't know how I've managed here without you!"

Eleanor smiled at her Dad and stroked Sweetpea's head.

"I've put a few closure strips on the wound. Sweetpea will be just fine in a few days – I think it looked worse than it really was," said Isobel. "She'll soon be back out there, chasing Gracie!" Gracie was their other goat, a Toggenburg.

Eleanor smiled at her mum and ran out into the sunshine. She walked slowly up to the old barn, now a tea room, and her tummy growled as she saw the slices of home-baked cakes lined up on the bright counter. Mrs. Cooper, her Gran, looked up as she spooned cream onto a strawberry scone.

"Hello, sweetheart! Do you know, I made far too many syrup flapjacks this morning. I wonder if you know anyone who could take some off my hands?"

Eleanor's face split in an enormous grin.

"You must have heard my tummy growling!" she said. "Can I take one for Alex and Beth too, please?"

Mrs. Cooper wrapped two crumbly flapjacks in a flowery napkin and gave them to Eleanor. The thick, syrupy smell made her mouth water.

"Thanks Grandma!" she cried happily as she ran off in search of her brother and sister.

★ top tip ★

Don't forget:

Skimming, scanning and key words (see pages 32–33)

Questions:

1. What bird do Eleanor and her mother see on the moors?

   _____.

2. Where had Eleanor been?

   _____.

3. Why does Kevin look anxious as Eleanor and Isobel enter the farmyard?

   _____.

4. What breed of goat is Sweetpea?

   _____.

5. Who is Gracie?

_____.

6. How does Isobel treat Sweetpea's injury?

_____.

7. Who is Mrs. Cooper?

_____.

8. What had Mrs. Cooper been doing that morning?

_____.

9. What are Eleanor's brother and sister called?

_____.

10. How do we know that Eleanor loves animals?

_____.

ANSWERS

NATIONAL TEST PRACTICE ANSWERS

Comprehension   **pages 90–92**

1. The bird they saw was a buzzard.

2. Eleanor had been visiting her Godmother, Hilary.

3. He looks anxious because Sweetpea, the goat, has cut her leg quite badly.

4. Sweetpea is an Angora goat.

5. Gracie is a Toggenburg goat.

6. Isobel puts closure strips on the wound to help it heal.

7. Mrs. Cooper is Eleanor's Grandma.

8. Mrs. Cooper has been baking flapjacks.

9. Eleanor's brother and sister are called Alex and Beth.

10. We know that Eleanor loves animals from the words, 'Eleanor's face glowed with excitement as she thought of the animals she would see that morning.' We are also told that she missed her pets whilst she was away.

TEST ROUND-UP ANSWERS

Test round-up   **pages 10–11**

Section 1

You were told to think about these questions:

1. ❖ Is uniform more or less expensive than ordinary
       clothes?
    ❖ You should have compared the prices of everyday
       clothes and school uniform.
2. ❖ Is uniform smart – and is being smart important?
    ❖ Why should we look smart for school?
    ❖ Does uniform help to make people look the same –
       and is that a good thing?
    ❖ What do kids wear at home?
    ❖ Do people tend to wear a casual uniform anyway? (jeans, trainers,
       sweat tops etc.)

Section 2

You should have a for and against table, filled in with details of your
research.

Section 3

You should have presented your arguments to an audience.

Comprehension Test – Test round-up   **pages 36–37**

Section 1 *Legend of Zelda – The Ocarina of Time*

1. Link
2. An evil wizard.
3. He wants to take control of the Tri force – the source of ultimate power.
4. Power, wisdom and bravery.
5. It will split into three parts.

Section 2 *The Black Death*

1. 1348
2. Men rather than women, young and strong rather than elderly and frail.
3. People carried sponges soaked in vinegar, and posies of flowers called
   'tussie-mussies' to ward off the plague fumes.
4. Fleas on rats.
5. Sneezing – a symptom of the plague.

Be an author – Test round-up   **pages 86–87**

You should have written a story for your chosen title. Did you include:

◆ Brainstorm   ◆ Story plan   ◆ Character profile
◆ Story starter   ◆ Strong ending

GLOSSARY

<u>Adjectives</u> Describing words that describe a noun.

<u>Adverbs</u> Describing words that modify a verb.

<u>Alliteration</u> When a sound is repeated in a sentence.

<u>Ambiguity</u> When the meaning is unclear, a sentence is said to be ambiguous.

<u>Appendix</u> A collection of extra information added at the end of a book.

<u>Autobiography</u> The story of a person's life, written by themselves.

<u>Biography</u> The story of a person's life, written by someone else.

<u>Blurb</u> Information given on the back of a book – often a short synopsis of part of the story.

<u>Brainstorm</u> First jottings of ideas when planning a piece of writing.

<u>Clause</u> A clause is a part of a sentence. It has a subject and a verb. It is not a sentence and does not have to start with a capital letter, or end with a full stop.

<u>Cliche</u> Cliches are words and phrases that have been used so many times that people get over-familiar – and bored – with them!

<u>Complex sentence</u> A complex sentence is built around a main clause and also has less important clauses.

<u>Compound sentence</u> Compound sentences have two important clauses. Each clause would make a simple sentence on its own, but can be joined to make a compound sentence.

<u>Conjunctions</u> Conjunctions are joining words. They are used to join other words and clauses. And, but, also, and because are all conjunctions.

<u>Consonant</u> All the letters of the alphabet except a e i o u

<u>Contractions</u> Contractions are words that have letters missing. An apostrophe shows where the letters have been missed out.

<u>CV, Curriculum Vitae</u> A record of work, interests and education that people use when they are applying for work.

<u>Debate</u> A reasoned argument between two teams of people.

<u>Fiction</u> Made-up stories and writing.

Footnote Notes at the bottom of a page that add extra explanations or information.

Formal writing Writing such as reports or formal letters.

Genre Horror, romance, science fiction – these are all genres.

Glossary Collection of useful words and their meanings.

Homophones Homophones sound the same, but mean different things. They are also spelled differently, like pear and pair.

Idiom Idioms are common phrases that are used and understood – but should not be taken literally!

Imagery Ways of making 'word pictures' – such as similes and metaphors.

Index An alphabetical list of contents in a book that helps the reader to find particular subjects.

Informal writing Writing to friends etc.

ISBN Number on the back of a book used to catalogue or order it.

Kennings A way of describing things without naming them.

Main clause The main clause is the most important part of the sentence, and contains the main idea. It would make sense on its own.

Metaphors A way of describing something by saying it IS something else – The moon WAS a tennis ball.

Mnemonic Making silly sentences or words to help you to remember things.

Narrator The narrator is the storyteller.

National Tests See SATs.

Non-fiction Factual writing such as found in a newspaper.

Noun A naming word – places, people, things.

Onomatopoeia A word that sounds like the thing it is describing, e.g. crash, bang.

Parenthesis Parenthesis means words that are added in brackets to a piece of writing to give us more information. Sometimes words in parenthesis are explanations, or they may be afterthoughts.

Personification When something is described by giving it human characteristics.

Plurals More than one.

Possessive apostrophes Apostrophes that show that something belongs to somebody or something.

Prefix Letters joined to the beginning of a word, e.g 'pre-' at the beginning of a word means 'before'.

Prepositions Prepositions are words that tell you the answer to the questions where and when. They tell you the relation between pronouns and nouns.

Pronouns Pronouns do the same job as nouns. Words like 'he', 'she', 'it', 'mine', and 'yours' are all pronouns. They are used in place of nouns.

Reported speech When someone tells us about what someone has said, rather than a person actually speaking.

SATs Standard Assessment Tests (also known as National Tests). In the primary school, SATs are carried out at the end of Key Stage One (at age 7) and at the end of Key Stage Two (at age 11). Tests are taken in English, Maths and Science.

Sequel A book written to continue the story begun in a previous book.

Similes Descriptions that say something is like something else – 'The sun was like an orange balloon.'

Simple sentence A simple sentence has one clause: The cat was grey.

Subordinate clause The less important clauses in sentences are called subordinate clauses. They do not make a sentence by themselves.

Helen ran quickly, because she saw the ice cream van.

main clause   subordinate clause

Suffix Letters joined at the end of a word, such as '-ing' or 'ed'.

Syllables Chunks of sound. Alligator has four syllables: all–ig–at–or.

Tense When something happens: Kicked – past tense. Kick/kicking – present tense. Shall kick – future tense.

Trilogy A set of three books (can also mean films and plays).

Verb An action or doing word.

Vowel The letters a e i o u. Every word in English has a vowel.